POCKET STUDY SKILLS

Kate Williams and Jude Carroll

REFERENCING
& UNDERSTANDING
PLAGIARISM

palgrave
macmillan

First published 2009 by
PALGRAVE MACMILLAN

Palgrave Macmillan in the UK is an imprint of Macmillan Publishers Limited, registered in England, company number 785998, of Houndmills, Basingstoke, Hampshire RG21 6XS.

Palgrave Macmillan in the US is a division of St Martin's Press LLC, 175 Fifth Avenue, New York, NY 10010.

Palgrave Macmillan is the global academic imprint of the above companies and has companies and representatives throughout the world.

Palgrave® and Macmillan® are registered trademarks in the United States, the United Kingdom, Europe and other countries

ISBN-13: 978-023-057479-3
ISBN-10: 0-230-57479-3

This book is printed on paper suitable for recycling and made from fully managed and sustained forest sources. Logging, pulping and manufacturing processes are expected to conform to the environmental regulations of the country of origin.

A catalogue record for this book is available from the British Library.

15 14 13 12 11 10
19 18 17 16 15 14

Printed in China

Contents

Acknowledgements

Many people have contributed, directly or indirectly, to this guide. First, our thanks go to students at Oxford Brookes University who brought us their struggles and triumphs with academic conventions. Special thanks to those who kindly allowed us to include extracts from their work. Thanks to Tom, whose dissertation and its references pointed to some absorbing sources, some of which have an echo in this guide.

We owe thanks to colleagues at Oxford Brookes University and elsewhere: colleagues at Upgrade study advice service; library staff who generously shared their expertise; and Kate's fellow authors of guides for students in the Schools of Health and Social Care and Education on how to reference. All helped to hone our thoughts about what students really need to know about referencing and understanding plagiarism. Thanks too to Sallie Godwin for her witty illustrations.

The author and publishers wish to thank the following for permission to reproduce copyright material: Oxfam, for their website; Elsevier for the article by Parkhurst and Lush; McGraw-Hill/OpenUniversity Press for use of Colin Neville's material; and Turnitin for use of their example.

Finally, our thanks to the editors at Palgrave Macmillan for their support and encouragement in producing this pocket guide, and for their hard work in making it happen.

Introduction

Welcome to this pocket guide! It's about how to reference (of course), and it explains plagiarism so that you never need worry about it again. We hope it does more than that, and shows you how to become a confident writer.

This guide is for anyone puzzled about referencing in universities in the UK, whether you come from work, school, or another country. We hope that reading it feels like a conversation, taking you through the thinking to the practicalities of what you put on your page.

The Pocket Study Skills series has been designed to fit in your pocket or bag, so you can take them with you anywhere. You may read whole sections of this guide (nothing is very long), but after that you are more likely to dip in and out, looking for examples, checking wording, models and advice. It is easy to see what's in it – flick through and you can see page by page.

Enjoy your research, and see yourself become a confident – and scholarly – writer.

Kate Williams
Jude Carroll

1 Writing at university

Reference?

This is not a reference. You do not refer to it.

Where did you get this from?

Too much quotation – not enough comment.

Your style isn't academic.

EVIDENCE??

Comments like these suggest two things:

- you need to get to grips with referencing
- you are not yet confident about how to draw on other writers and sources in your own writing.

This guide is about both of these. The first, referencing, is relatively straightforward. You need to get your head around what referencing is, and why it is such an important practice at university. Then, find out which style of referencing your tutors want you to use. And use it – simple as that.

The point about confidence is trickier. You need confidence in using the conventions of academic writing in your subject area. Again, once you know what these conventions are and understand why they are used, you will be able to reference and write with confidence.

And plagiarism? When you really understand how to draw on other people's ideas and words, then the problem of plagiarism just disappears. It will be your own work that you hand in and you will get credit for it. You will be confident of your ability to write from sources and your tutors will feel the same.

What's different about writing at university?

Quite a lot. That's true no matter where you studied before. Nor is it easy to explain exactly why writing at university is different …

Universities are research environments. Most tutors and lecturers do research of some sort and base their writing on the style used in the books, articles and reports they read for their research: that's where they, too, publish. So it follows that students are also expected to develop the 'academic' style that matches their field of study.

So what is UK 'academic' style?

Well, of course it varies from subject to subject – after all, dance, science and business are massively different, so the style of writing expected in different areas of study will vary too. But let's try a few generalisations!

You are NOT expected to:
▶ write out facts, describe events, and just summarise your reading or lectures (unless you are expressly asked to – for example, to draw up a timeline, outline, describe a process or observation or do a 'summary').

You ARE expected to:
▶ consider a question or topic from several angles: if you are asked to 'outline' different theories, studies or interpretations of 'facts' or events, you will almost certainly be expected to 'discuss' or 'evaluate' them too.

You are ALWAYS expected to:
▶ Show the EVIDENCE for the statements you make. You will need evidence if the statement is a 'fact', or mentions the approach of a particular writer, or describes the findings of a study.

So on to referencing …

You provide evidence by telling the reader about the source of your information. The reference is the link between what you write and the evidence on which your writing is based. It turns what you write from being just your thoughts and reactions to something that links your ideas with the writings of other people who have thought about the same issue.

Reference, reference, reference – why do I have to reference everything?

There is one overarching reason why you need to reference: a reference tells your reader where the evidence for what you say has come from (see also p. 59).

Readers can then use your reference in different ways. They can:

1 go and find the source themselves if they want to
2 understand the nature of your source
3 form their own view about the use you make of it.

And, of course, if your reader is a tutor, s/he can see what you have read and what sources you have used for your assignment. That helps them to assess the quality of your work and the range of your research.

Help your reader to find your source!

It isn't good enough just to list everything you have read for an assignment at the end of your writing. At best this just tells your reader that you've been busy; at worst it gives the impression that you've borrowed a list from somewhere else. Plus, you can't expect your reader to wade through 5, 15 or 50 sources to try and find that nugget of information you have used. They will just get annoyed ('where did she get this from?') – and you will be the loser.

The whole purpose of referencing is to make the process of tracking back to previous research as clear as possible. **Point** your reader to where they can find the source or support for particular statements.

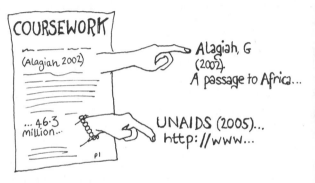

Make it easy! A good source can be a goldmine for someone who is interested in your topic. It could lead them to a whole network of sources that in turn could help them in their research.

All referencing systems have two linked elements

In the text you drop in a signal at the point in your writing where you are using a source. This is a 'citation', a link that tells the reader two things: first, that the idea or information comes from elsewhere, and secondly, where to look for more information on that source. The signal is either:

> *If it's in my text it's in my reference list. If it's in my reference list it's in my text.*

▶ a number in numeric systems[1] or [1]; or
▶ the author + year (in most author-date systems).

In the 'references' section you list ALL your sources, giving full details of where to find them. The list can be either:

▶ in number order according to where you first use that source in your text; or
▶ in alphabetical order by the author's last name. Whichever style you use …

There needs to be 100% correspondence between the sources you
▶ use (or 'cite') in your text; and
▶ list at the end with full tracking details in your references list.

For the difference between 'References' and a 'Bibliography' see p. 77.

What does your reader need to know? The bare essentials

The questions your reader needs answers to are:

Who wrote it?

When was it published?

What is the **title** of the article?

What journal was it published in?

Where exactly can I find it?

The answers you need to give in your reference are:

Justin Parkhurst and Louisiana Lush wrote an article (published) in **2004**. It is **'The political environment of HIV: lessons from a comparison of Uganda and South Africa'**. It was published in the journal **Social Science and Medicine**, in **volume 59, issue 9** on **pages 1913–24**.

In reference form (author-year Harvard style), this becomes:

1 Author(s)   *2 Year*   *3 Title of article*

Parkhurst JO and Lush L (2004). The political environment of HIV: lessons from a comparison of Uganda and South Africa. *Social Science and Medicine*. 59(9), p1913–24.

           4 Title of journal

5 Volume + Issue   *6 Pages*

All referencing styles provide details that answer the same questions – they are just set out differently.

Styles of referencing

There are several main styles of referencing and plenty of local variations. There are differences so tiny that even specialists struggle to spot the difference. Add to this the house styles favoured by individual journal and book publishers and individual tutors' quirks, and there are probably hundreds of different variations in use around the world – all perfectly correct.

Different disciplines tend to have their preferred way of referencing, often with good reason, sometimes by convention. As a newcomer to the subject, clearly you should follow the models. However, even within one subject area – sometimes even in the same department – there can be differences. Individual tutors tend to want students to set out references in the way they themselves do.

All this makes for conflicting advice and confusion for students. What's OK on one module can be marked as wrong on another. The upshot is that referencing has become a real bugbear for many people, and, worse still, students (and tutors!) often fail to distinguish between what is important in referencing and what is not.

They are all correct!

There are plenty of variations within any referencing style with individual preferences and house styles creating their own. Here is a sample of styles – and they would all be classified as the 'Harvard' style.

> PARKHURST, J.O. and L. LUSH (2004). The political environment of HIV: lessons from a comparison of Uganda and South Africa. *Social Science and Medicine*. No 59(9), p1913–24.
>
> Parkhurst, J.O. and Lush, L. 2004. The Political Environment of HIV: lessons from a comparison of Uganda and South Africa. <u>Social Science and Medicine</u>. Vol. 59, issue 9, pp. 1913–24.
>
> Parkhurst JO and Lush L (2004). 'The political environment of HIV: lessons from a comparison of Uganda and South Africa'. *Soc Sci Med*. **59**(9): 1913–24.

They have all been modelled on books and articles published by major publishers and they are all absolutely correct!

So what do you do?

Try a bit of self-preservation! Find out how your reader wants you to reference – and set out your references in the way your reader – tutor or editor – wants them set out.

Your module/course handbook will almost certainly state how they want this done. Keep your handbook handy when you are writing, and follow the models. Exactly.

What matters and what doesn't?

It doesn't matter if you:

▶ use or don't use commas, full stops, capitals in titles, underlining/italics. But be consistent because playing too fast and loose with punctuation annoys readers;

▶ can't track down some detail, despite your best efforts. It's better to refer to a good source than to leave it out because of a missing detail.

It does matter that you:

▶ understand the purpose of referencing

▶ place your in-text reference (or 'citation') at the point you use a source

▶ give as full a set of details as you can about each source in your reference list

▶ develop ways of weaving references into your writing style in your own way

▶ give up the idea of 'hanging on' to the words used in your source, even if you feel they say it better than you do

▶ pick one style of referencing and stick to it.

It is unrealistic, however, to expect students to be 100% accurate. World-class professors send books and articles to publishers with incomplete references and copy-editors check and correct missing reference details. Tutors will be looking for authenticity – wanting to see what you have really read and thought about this source material.

Most courses will use a style from one of the two 'families' below, or local adaptations of these. You don't need to know them all – check the ones used in the courses you take.

Family 1: In-text name styles

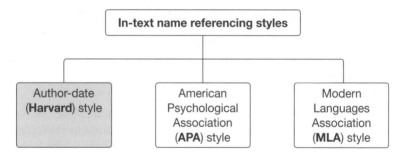

Source: Neville, *The Complete Guide to Referencing and Avoiding Plagiarism* (OpenUniversity Press, 2007), p43.

In your text you cite the surname of the author(s), and the year of the publication (for Harvard and APA) at the point at which you draw on a source (MLA is a little different – see p. 104). For example:

> In terms of economic power, recent civil strife, geographics and demographics, and existing infrastructure, Uganda was not notably advanced beyond its neighbours (Parkhurst and Lush 2004).

In your reference list at the end of your essay, you set out the full details of where to find the article, so your reader can track back and find it. You list all your sources in alphabetical order, by (first) author's surname. For example:

> Parkhurst JO and Lush L (2004). The political environment of HIV: lessons from a comparison of Uganda and South Africa. *Social Science and Medicine*. 59(9), p1913–24.

This guide uses Harvard except where we explicitly state that we are giving examples of other styles. Other styles are outlined in Part 3.

Family 2: In-text numerical styles

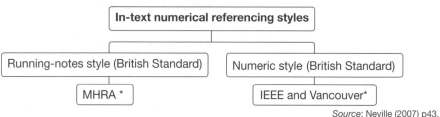

Source: Neville (2007) p43.

In your text you use a number, in superscript[3] or brackets, round (3) or square [3] to show the point at which you draw on a source. For example:

> In terms of economic power, recent civil strife, geographics and demographics, and existing infrastructure, Uganda was not notably advanced beyond its neighbours[3].

In your reference list, you list your references in numbered order, with the first source you use listed as 1, the second as 2 and so on. For example:

> 3   Parkhurst JO and Lush L. The political environment of HIV: lessons from a comparison of Uganda and South Africa. *Social Science and Medicine*. 2004, 59(9) p1913–24.

The numerical styles are most used in science, medicine and related areas. Some numerical styles are outlined on pp. 105–8 .

*not outlined in this guide

4 Referencing in action – a student at work

This section shows an extract from the introduction to a 3rd-year undergraduate dissertation. The writer, Tom, uses references in a way that shows exactly where he got his information from. He leaves clear footprints:

▶ in his text, at the exact point where he uses each source, taking you to

▶ where to find each source yourself, from the full reference list at the back.

3 UGANDA AND THE AIDS CRISIS

3.1 Uganda: the Political, Economic and Demographic context to the HIV/AIDS crisis

Uganda obtained independence from Britain in 1962. The removal of colonial rule left a power vacuum, precipitating a long period of political instability. Milton Obote twice ruled the country, either side of the eight year Idi Amin dictatorship (1971–79). This turbulent period was one of minimal economic growth (Human Development Reports 2005) and volatile politics. International relations remained soured until the emergence of greater stability and national unity, and economic reform under Yoweri Museveni, President since 1986 (Alagiah 2002).

In 1986, when Museveni recognised that Uganda had a problem with HIV, Uganda was comparable to many other sub-Saharan countries. In terms of economic power, recent civil strife, geographics and demographics, and existing infrastructure, Uganda was not notably advanced beyond its neighbours (Parkhurst and Lush 2004). Uganda started its fight against HIV with limited resources, and no indication that it should fare any better than surrounding countries. For this reason, it is crucial to examine what occurred in Uganda to make it stand out from its neighbours as a possible model for fighting HIV in a limited resource environment.

3.2 HIV in Africa and Uganda

It is estimated that in 2005 there were 40.3 million people living with HIV/AIDS globally (UNAIDS 2005). The most affected region in the world is sub-Saharan Africa which …

Here are the references Tom used in this extract, Harvard style, in alphabetical order by author:

References

Alagiah G (2002). *A Passage to Africa.* London: Time Warner Paperbacks.

Human Development Reports (2005). *Human Development Report 2005.* Available at http://hdr.undp.org/reports/global/2005/pdf/HDR05_HDI.pdf [Accessed 20/01/06].

Parkhurst JO and Lush L (2004). The political environment of HIV: lessons from a comparison of Uganda and South Africa. *Social Science and Medicine.* 59(9) p1913–24.

UNAIDS (2005). *AIDS epidemic update: December 2005.* Geneva: UNAIDS. Available at http://www.unaids.org/epi/2005/doc/EPIupdate2005_pdf_en/Epi05_02_en.pdf [Accessed 13/01/06]

The test! Tracking Tom's research footprints

Remember why the reader needs a reference (p. 5)?

1 Can I find the source?
2 What kind of source is it?
3 How does the author use it?

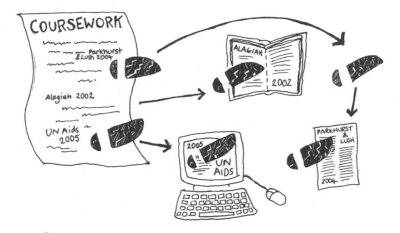

How easy is it for the reader to follow the trail?

Source 1 (Alagiah)

Finding it: Easy. It's there in the library catalogue, and there on the shelf.

What kind of source? A book. It's an engrossing personal reflective account, not exactly a historical text.

Well used? Yes. Authoritative enough for the author's purpose.

Source 2 (Human Development Reports)

Finding it: The link didn't work. A quick google for 'Human Development Reports' and there it is, 'December HDR2005' – but the HDI (Human Development Indicators) where this information came from was right at the back (p. 211 onwards!). Page numbers would have helped.

What kind of source? An excellent primary source – a report. Authoritative, relevant, reliable.

Well used? Definitely. Spot on as a source of data.

Source 3 (Parkhurst & Lush)

Finding it: With the full reference details this should be easy – year (2004), Volume (59),

Issue (9), and pages (1913–1924) – and it was, both electronically and in the 2004 box on the library shelf.

What kind of source? A highly reliable academic, peer-reviewed journal.

(Every article in a 'peer reviewed' journal has been read and checked by specialists in the specific research area before publication.)

Well used? Spot on for the author's purpose.

Source 4 (UNAIDS)

Finding it: Perfect – straight through to the 'Global summary of the AIDS epidemic'.

(By the time you read this, it may have moved, but with the full publication details including place of publication it should be easy to locate.)

What kind of source? UNAIDS website – the primary source for information of this sort. Highly authoritative.

Well used? Figure well used to introduce a point.

Take-away points

Conventional hard copy sources exist in time and space – that's great when your library holds them.

Reputable academic journals accessed electronically will also go back a long time. The electronic version (in pdf) will normally look like the original article, be safely stored, and not move around like online materials often do.

Online materials tend to move around, as organisations constantly update and redesign their websites. So you need to:

▶ Give your reader as much information as possible – give all the details as for a hard copy, in case they need to search for it.

▶ Show the date you accessed it like this: [Accessed 13/01/06]. This tells your reader, 'It was there then – even if it isn't there now.' It will probably still be somewhere on the site if it's a reputable source (as with Source 2 above).

▶ Copy URLs using 'cut and paste'. One tiny error with manual copying could mean your source can't be found.

The research process

Collecting your sources and recording your references systematically starts way back, well before you start writing.

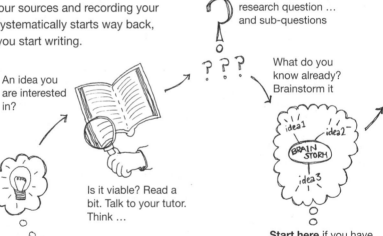

Ask a specific research question … and sub-questions

An idea you are interested in?

What do you know already? Brainstorm it

idea1
idea2
BRAIN STORM
idea3

Is it viable? Read a bit. Talk to your tutor. Think …

Start here if you choose your topic.

Start here if you have been set a question

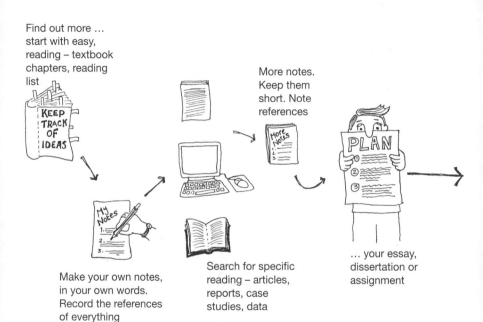

Find out more … start with easy, reading – textbook chapters, reading list

KEEP TRACK OF IDEAS

More notes. Keep them short. Note references

More Notes

PLAN

My Notes

Make your own notes, in your own words. Record the references of everything

Search for specific reading – articles, reports, case studies, data

… your essay, dissertation or assignment

Transforming sources into ideas

When you approach your research systematically, and make notes as you go, you will find that the materials you find and read gradually shape and transform your thinking. The ideas taking shape in your head have roots that go back into the material you have read. Readers want to see both the roots of your ideas, and the value you have added in thinking about them.

See the writer thinking

A good writer is always thinking, using ideas and facts from sources to shape and inform an argument. Readers need to see the roots of an idea in a source and then see how the writer uses it. Where does s/he take it?

The extract from Tom's work (p. 16) is an apparently factual bit of background information about Uganda. What clues do you see about this writer's thoughts on what he has read?

Tom wrote …	The reader sees …
In terms of economic power, recent civil strife, geographics and demographics, and existing infrastructure, Uganda was not notably advanced beyond its neighbours (Parkhurst and Lush 2004). Uganda started its fight against HIV with limited resources, and no indication that it should fare any better than surrounding countries.	You can hear Tom's voice: his comments 'not notably advanced', and 'no indication that it should fare any better' summarise a much longer section in the article by Parkhurst and Lush.
For this reason, it is crucial to examine what occurred in Uganda to make it stand out from its neighbours as a possible model for fighting HIV in a limited resource environment.	Here Tom takes the next step. He is stepping off the source, to set out his own argument, telling the reader why his research is important.

Why use the research of other authors?

You may want to:
- use an author as an authority to support what you are saying
- introduce someone else's perspective that you want to discuss
- provide evidence of a trend or development you are discussing
- show differences between experts' views and interpretations
- show the difference between an author's views and your own.

And when do you need to reference?

You need to reference when you:
- use facts, figures or specific details you pick from somewhere to support a point you're making – you **report**
- use a framework or model another author has devised. Let's say you **'acknowledge'**
- use the exact words of your source – you **quote**

- restate in your own words a specific point, finding or argument an author has made – you **paraphrase**
- sum up in a phrase or a few sentences a whole article or chapter, a key finding/conclusion, or a section – you **summarise**.

You don't need to reference if you:

- believe that what you are writing is widely known and accepted by all as 'fact'. This is usually called 'common knowledge'
- can honestly say, 'I didn't have to research anything to know that!'.

But

If finding it out did take effort, show the reader the research you did by referencing it.

Try this!

If you write something down which you can imagine someone else asking questions about, like 'Really?' 'Who says?' 'Why's that?' 'That's a lot!' 'How do you know that?' … then you must have found it out from somewhere, and you should show your reader where it comes from – in a reference.

Report

When you report on specific information you have found and which you now need to use – like a fact, event, figure, map or date – you bring it into your text, and

- give the in-text reference (or 'citation')
- give the full reference in the references section.

In your text	In your references
It is estimated that in 2005 there were 40.3 million people living with HIV/AIDS globally (UNAIDS 2005).	UNAIDS (2005). *AIDS epidemic update: December 2005.* Geneva: UNAIDS. Available at http://www.unaids.org/epi/2005/doc/EPIupdate2005_pdf_en/Epi05_02_en.pdf [Accessed 13/01/06]
The eco-tourism market is set to increase markedly in the next few years: from 450,000 holidays in 2005 to 2.5 million trips in 2010 (Mintel 2005).	Mintel (2005) Ethical Holidays UK. October. Available at http://academic.mintel.com/sinatra/oxygen_academic/search_results/show&/display/id=125548 [Accessed 22 March 2008]

Acknowledge

We found Colin Neville's way of categorising referencing styles really useful (pp. 12, 14), and have used his 'framework' in this guide. It has helped us to organise this text, so it is important that we acknowledge the source. There is also something about 'good manners' in acknowledging a debt to the person who came up with a model, template or framework – even, or especially, if you then develop or change it, as we did with the description 'family trees'.

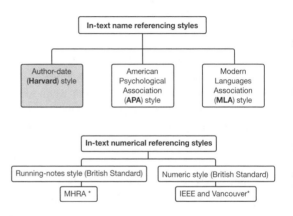

Source: Neville, *The Complete Guide to Referencing and Avoiding Plagiarism* (OpenUniversity Press, 2007), p43.

Quote

'To copy out or repeat (a passage, statement etc) from a book, document, speech etc with some indication that one is giving the words of another'.

Source: The Shorter Oxford English Dictionary (1983)

Only use a quote when it is especially important for your reader to see and appreciate the precise wording of the original. You may decide to do this:

▶ to provide the reader with the original when you are discussing the text in detail (like in poetry, literary or historical criticism, regulations, policy documents);
▶ because the writer (or speaker) is eminent/surprising/authoritative;
▶ because the words themselves are vivid/surprising/a catchphrase and you'd lose the impact if you tried to explain or paraphrase it.

Use quotations sparingly. Quoted extracts – other people's words – are not an alternative to explaining a point in your own words and your own language.

Example:

> George Orwell's advice to writers is as relevant today as it was in the England of the 1940s: 'Never use a long word where a short word will do.' (Orwell 1946 p169). In the 21st century, students …

Short quotations (less than two lines)

To use short quotes well:

- run the quotation into your text so that it reads smoothly
- use quotation marks, single or double, as long as you are consistent
- give the page number of the original in your in-text reference, so your reader can find it easily
- give the full reference in your references section.

Example:

> Ofsted described schools' approach to sustainability as 'piecemeal and uncoordinated', although specific teaching was often 'excellent' (Ofsted 2008 p4). This raises the question of how …

Example:

> Charlotte Smith has been accused of having 'a happy knack of exploiting popular taste' (Wu 2006 p76). This could be a little harsh. It could simply be …

Quotation marks are used so your reader can distinguish at a glance between your words and the words of the other writer (or speaker). Your quote must use the exact wording, punctuation and spelling of the original.

Long quotations (two lines or more)

Typically a long quotation is used for an extract from a key text (for example, a policy document) you want to discuss. Try to avoid going above five lines of original text – readers find long extracts too distracting when they are trying to follow your ideas. To use long quotes well:

▸ indent the passage – so no need for quotation marks (don't use them);
▸ give the in-text link (citation) to the reference list at the end of the quotation (author-date or numeric), and the page number(s) of the original;
▸ give the full reference in the references section.

Example:

> The Prime Minister introduced the government's strategy to tackle obesity in these terms:
>> Our ambition is to be the first major nation to reverse the rising tide of obesity […] by ensuring that everyone is able to achieve and maintain a healthy weight. Our initial focus will be on children: by 2020 we aim to reduce the proportion of overweight and obese children to 2000 levels. (Department of Health 2008 p2)
> It is worth noting that the obesity levels of 2000 are now …

[…] shows some words have been left out of the quotation.

If you decide to leave out some words in a quoted extract, you can add words in square brackets to make the extract read smoothly.

Example:

> The government's strategy to tackle obesity focuses initially on children:
>> Our ambition is to be the first major nation to reverse the rising tide of obesity [particularly in] children: by 2020 we aim to reduce the proportion of overweight and obese children to 2000 levels (Department of Health 2008 p2). Obesity levels in 2000 have become the benchmark for ... and raises the question ...

Quote + comment

The key thing about deciding to use a quote is:

> If it's worth a quote, it's worth a comment!

Don't just drop a quote and run off to your next point. Tell your reader why you think those words are special: what the quote might mean, how it is interpreted, what is interesting/surprising/new/influential about the quoted comment. This doesn't have to be a big deal – see the examples above.

Using sources in your writing

Too much quoting

Generally students quote too much, and comment too little. Do you?

Try this!

▸ Ask yourself: *Are these words (or this extract) somehow special?* If it isn't, then report it, paraphrase it, summarise it – plus comment on it!

▸ Read a couple of pages from journal articles on your reading list. Count the quotes. Not many? This is telling you something.

As a rule of thumb, if you find yourself quoting more than a couple of words more than once or twice per side (unless it's a piece of writing where quoting is half the point, such as an essay about poetry, or discussing a policy document), or if you find yourself taking a couple of lines from any one source more than once or twice, then you are probably overdoing the quotes. Try and find another way to include the point or discussion.

Paraphrase

'To express the meaning of (a word, phrase etc) in other words'.

Source: The Shorter Oxford English Dictionary (1983)

Paraphrase is about expressing the **meaning** of short extracts – the definition suggests a single word or a short phrase, but it can be longer than this. To express meaning in your own words you first have to understand it, and then find the words to express it.

Paraphrase is hard work. Keep it for short extracts, when the idea is useful to your argument or what you want to say, but the words are not special. Where the words are special, quote (briefly) + comment.

When you paraphrase:

- pick out the key point from the original you want to pay close attention to
- use your own words to restate what the author is saying
- aim to end up with a shorter version than the original
- put the in-text reference as close as you can to your paraphrase, and give the page number(s) of the original
- list the full details in the references
- tell your reader what you want them to see in it – don't just drop it there in the text and run off to your next point!

Example

Jay wrote ...	The reader sees ...
Eriksen (1993) comments that the term 'race' is of 'dubious descriptive value' (p4), first, because so many people in the world are of mixed race, and second, because the variation within a single 'racial' group (Eriksen's punctuation) is greater than the variation between different groups.	A close paraphrase of a short paragraph. Key words are quoted (they are 'special' – they sum up the author's view), and Jay explains the two reasons in his own words. The reasons are important to understand, but the words of the original are not. Plus, he has shortened it.

Problems with paraphrase often arise when students try to capture summaries by other authors and re-express them in their own words. A textbook or article may summarise the findings or arguments of other studies so that the reader gets an overview of debates or research in that field. The problem for you, the reader, is that you haven't read these other studies, so you don't know what they say (apart from what the text in front of you says they say).

Here paraphrasing takes on a whole new dimension. Students can find themselves trying to repeat someone else's summary, wondering how many words they have to change (one in four? one in ten?) for it to become their 'own' and not be detected by a text-matching software package such as Turnitin. Or they give up and cut-and-paste.

Don't go there! Be very sparing with paraphrase. Summarise bigger sections, report on specific findings, and quote + comment on special words. And always show where the ideas came from with a reference.

See p. 79 for how to reference a source you find summarised in what you are reading.
See p. 69–71 for what counts as plagiarism.

Summarise

'To state briefly or succinctly'.

Source: The Shorter Oxford English Dictionary (1983)

Summary is key. It is the most efficient way of capturing your research in your writing. Use it if you want to capture, for example:

▶ key outcomes of a study
▶ an argument
▶ the approach taken to …

First, do your reading. Read a page or two. Look up and think: 'What, in a nutshell, does this tell me that I can use in what I am saying?'

Then write it down, in your own words. Keep it short.

Key steps in making a summary

▶ Pick out the key points from the original.
▶ Make your own notes, in your own words. When you also include phrases from the original, put them in quotes in your notes. Add what you think is important about the point or quote to remind yourself when you come back to it.
▶ Record full details of each source.

Then, when you write:

▶ use your own words (of course! The original will be far too long!)
▶ put the in-text reference as close as you can to the summary (before or after)
▶ list the full details in the references
▶ if you are capturing meaning that arises from several pages of reading, you don't need to give page numbers. If you are summarising a short bit, then give the page number(s) of where exactly you got it from.

Summarising key findings

Opposite on the left is an extract from a journal article that shows how experienced researchers summarise – in very few words – key findings from other articles in the field to provide evidence for the argument they are making.

The authors wrote ...	The reader sees ...
In sub-Saharan Africa, nurses commonly bear the brunt of health-care delivery, but their numbers have declined substantially in recent years because of migration. In Malawi, for example, there has been a 12% reduction in available nurses due to migration (Ross et al. 2005). In 2000, roughly 500 nurses left Ghana, double the number of nursing graduates for that same year (Awases et al. 2004). The recent upsurge in migration has affected the ability of nurse training programmes to continue because of poor staffing levels (Dovlo 2007). Death caused by infectious and chronic diseases (Tawfik and Kinoti 2003) is also a major contributor to nurse attrition in the region.	In this first sentence (the 'topic sentence') the writers make a clear statement of *their* point. Then they support their point with evidence from four studies: a study about Malawi, a study about Ghana a study about training programmes a study about the impact of disease – which links back directly to the authors' point about declining numbers of nurses in sub-Saharan Africa.
Source: Mills et al. (2008 p685)	It's a well-written paragraph!

Each paragraph in Mills et al.'s article develops one point. String these together, and a series of well-supported and evidenced points quickly becomes an argument.

Summarising shorter sections

You don't have to summarise whole articles in just a few words, of course! You can summarise any material you want to use, with any level of detail you choose. But the process is the same. Ask yourself: what is it they are saying, in a nutshell? Is it useful to me? Then bring the point into your work, re-express it in your own words, show where it came from, and comment on it.

Regina at work

Regina is writing an essay on the recruitment and retention of healthcare professionals in the NHS. She is interested in the argument of Mills and colleagues: that recruitment of health workers from poor African countries should be viewed as a crime. A crime? This is strong stuff! Before she draws on their work she has some questions to ask. What evidence do they build their arguments on? How do they justify their position? She wants to give her reader a more detailed account of their argument.

Regina wrote …	The reader sees …
Mills et al. (2008) argue that current levels of migration from sub-Saharan Africa to developed countries will have 'dire' (p687) consequences for health in Africa. Based on known patterns of migration in 2004, they project worsening ratios of physicians, nurses and pharmacists 2006–2012 in a population with rising healthcare needs caused by the increase in numbers of people with HIV. In this context Mills at al. describe the loss of skilled personnel through active recruitment by affluent Western countries as 'a violation of the human rights of people in Africa' (p687), and point to various declarations to underline the moral and possibly legal case for ethical recruitment …	Regina's summary of Mills et al.'s argument: <u>her</u> main point about the 'dire' consequences (strong word, quoted) is in the topic sentence. She summarises a table and a chart to pick out the key messages about loss of skilled nurses; and adds in a point from the article about HIV. She mentions Mills et al. again by name to remind us that we are still reading a summary of their research, and quotes a key phrase. She doesn't list all the policies and legal agreements, but focuses on the way Mills et al. use them to make their argument …

Summary is *the* most useful skill in writing about your research. Combined with short quotes it gives a powerful flavour of the research you are reading, and offers a ready way for you to draw material into your argument.

7 Write with confidence

Putting references in your text

As soon as your reader starts thinking these things, then as a writer you have a problem. You need to get in quicker and show your reader whose ideas you are writing about.

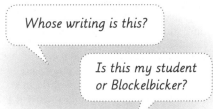

Whose writing is this?

Is this my student or Blockelbicker?

Where is this coming from?

Try this:

▶ Show your source before your reader starts to wonder whose work they're reading!

And:

▶ If your account of what an author said continues for more than one sentence, repeat the author's name as a reminder to your reader that they are reading your version of what someone else says.

Look at the example above of Regina. Halfway down, she puts in a reminder that she is still talking about Mills et al.'s research.

Two styles for writing

Style 1: Focus on the *ideas*

In this writing style, you want to focus on the ideas and research findings that provide evidence for your argument. You add the author(s) and year in brackets to show the reader where ideas come from. The brackets hardly interrupt the flow, and academic readers are well used to this.

Below is the extract about nurse migration from sub-Saharan Africa (p. 39) The key points are shown in **bold**, and the in-text references are just there.

> In sub-Saharan Africa, **nurses** commonly bear the brunt of health-care delivery, but their **numbers have declined** substantially in recent years because of migration. In Malawi, for example, there has been a 12% reduction in available nurses due to **migration** (Ross et al. 2005). In 2000, roughly **500 nurses left Ghana**, double the number of nursing graduates for that same year (Awases et al. 2004). The recent upsurge in migration has affected the ability of **nurse training programmes** to continue because of poor staffing levels (Dovlo 2007). **Death caused by infectious and chronic diseases** is also a major contributor to nurse attrition in the region (Tawfik and Kinoti 2003).

Source: Mills et al. (2008 p685) with bold added for emphasis.

Style 2: Focus on the *source*

In this writing style, you want the reader to be more aware of the authors/researchers (as well as their findings or ideas) and you use their names as a natural part of the text. You add the year in brackets to pinpoint the sources listed in the reference list. You also need to use words to introduce the research – also shown in bold.

In sub-Saharan Africa, nurses commonly bear the brunt of health-care delivery, but their numbers have declined substantially in recent years because of migration. **Ross et al. (2005) found** that in Malawi, there has been a 12% reduction in available nurses due to migration. **Awases et al. (2004) calculated** that in 2000, roughly 500 nurses left Ghana, double the number of nursing graduates for that same year. **Dovlo (2007) describes the impact of** the recent upsurge in migration on the ability of nurse training programmes to continue and **attributes** poor staffing levels **to** this migration. Death caused by infectious and chronic diseases has been **identified by Tawfik and Kinoti (2003)** as a major contributor to nurse attrition in the region.

Source: Mills et al. (2008 p685), minor amendments, and bold added.

Your choice

When you write, use whichever style seems to fit most naturally in your sentence, and feel free to move between them in the same piece of writing.

The wordcount factor

▶ Style 2 (focus on the source) is about 10% longer than Style 1.
▶ Style 1 (focus on the ideas) is about 10% longer than the numeric style (see p. 105–6).

These figures are inflated because we have used the extracts to illustrate points, but it is worth noticing that numerical referencing styles are generally more economical with words.

Words to introduce sources

Notice the language used to introduce the various studies and their authors:

> X found that ... ; calculated that ... ; describes the impact of ... ;
> attributes to ... ; identified by ...

All these studies seem to be pretty clear about their conclusions, and they all confirm the same trend. The writers are using them to provide evidence for their argument – so the language here is quite definite.

How sure are you?

How do researchers report on their findings?

Researchers are very careful about their use of language when they write up their research.

Tentative	**Definite**
Emerging research	Established findings

When 'new knowledge' begins to emerge, researchers are very cautious and tentative about their conclusions, and only make statements for which they feel the evidence is solid:

> *There is the possibility that …*
> *… also suggests that …*
> *X (2001) feels that …*
> *Studies in … indicate that …*

As knowledge in a field becomes more established, the debate moves on:

> *Dissenbak (2005) maintains …*
> *Two recent studies (Clogg and Klee, 2006; Ballard, 2004)*
> *challenge …*
> *According to X (2002) …*

And as 'knowledge' becomes confirmed by further studies, more categorical statements can be made:

> *X (2006) found that … / demonstrated that … / showed …*

The key point here for you is: DON'T OVERSTATE! Only be as definite in your language as the evidence allows you to be.

And if you want to show differences …?

If you want to show differences between the views and interpretations of experts in the field, or between an author's views and your own, there are ways of showing how close or distant you are to the views or findings of an author.

Distant	Close
Cohn (2001) claims that …	
discussed the idea that …	
considers that …	
contends that … observed	
points out that …	
asserts … reported that	
states that …	
has shown / demonstrated that …	
confirms that …	

Or you keep a neutral style

According to …

X reports on … argues that …

This explains …

Your sources, your friends!

The writers who inform your thinking – provide you with information, facts and figures, give you case studies to draw on, and material for your arguments – are your friends!

In the same way that you might (in theory at least!) record who said what in a discussion about a film over coffee, you need to be careful to attribute who said what in your writing.

Enjoy the discussion!

PART 2

UNDERSTANDING PLAGIARISM

8 Plagiarism and academic integrity

Part 2 is the flip side of Part 1. It focuses on the difference between when students write as authors, and when students copy other people's work and present it as their own. That's plagiarism.

When people plagiarise at university they don't show where the ideas and information they use came from – they just copy. Students who don't use referencing conventions run the risk of their tutors thinking they might be plagiarising – hence the link.

Of course, some plagiarism is deliberate. Students who pay someone to do the work or blatantly cut and paste or copy others' work have not learnt anything. When they hand in work, they are claiming 'Here's my assignment'. Quite plainly it isn't, and quite plainly this is cheating. This guide is not about that sort of plagiarism.

This guide is for students who do their own work and want to take credit for it, but are worried that they don't understand plagiarism and might slip into it by accident. Part 2 explains why universities are so bothered about plagiarism and how student writers can be sure that the P-word will never be attached to their work.

Academic integrity and plagiarism – some definitions

Being told 'Don't plagiarise' is like saying 'Don't break the rules'. This is pointless unless students know what those rules are and why they are there. So now, universities start with their values and beliefs in a statement of 'Academic Integrity'.

Typically, a university statement about academic integrity will say something like this:

> Your work should be truthful and ethical; it should mean what you say it means. It should reflect your own efforts and insights. And it should acknowledge and value others' work, too, which, in this context, means citing their work truthfully and showing how your own work builds on theirs.

Students are expected to work according to these values even if they do not themselves (yet!) share them.

Plagiarism is part of the bigger picture of academic integrity

> Plagiarism happens when you submit someone else's work as your own.

9 'It's my own work'. What does that mean?

Many courses require students to sign a sheet saying the work is their own. You must have ticked dozens of boxes on websites to say you've read the terms and conditions (really?). But what are you signing up to when you sign 'This is my work'?

WORK not words!

We are talking about WORK here, not just about words. Part 1 described some of the work involved in writing good assignments: identifying sources, taking notes, linking your sources with your points and arguments ... for starters. Then there's the work of turning your ideas into words and the work of putting the whole thing together as a cogent piece of text. All that most definitely adds up to WORK!

This is what you are being assessed on. This is what you take credit for – and this is a major route by which you learn.

Learning: the point of it all

Tutors design courses, assignments and 'learning experiences' which they think will promote learning. They also have to make sure the rules are followed and that anyone who gets credit for achieving something does so by the rules and plays fair.

The 'rules of the university game' might be explained like this:

> We don't give credit for students doing the assignment, we give credit if students learn something by doing the work we set.

What's the difference?

Look at the following two tables to see the difference.

A student hands in an assignment that shows ...	What's going on?
'I took care of seven people with emphysema.'	That's doing something. OK, but that's all it is.
'I took care of seven patients with emphysema and here is a care plan about the best ways to take care of patients with emphysema which I found in my textbook.'	That's not learning, that's doing something and copying. And they don't connect. Is the care any better for having read the textbook? There's no evidence of it.
'Two months ago, I could not have made a care plan for a patient with emphysema. Now I have taken care of seven and read some books and talked with people who know about it and, now, here's my care plan.'	That's learning, and the plan shows the work that went into the learning. It is based on the evidence of other people's work in the field, informing your own ideas and approach.

A student describes what she did for her assignment …	What's going on?
'I found a really good website about sustainable tourism and another one about Sri Lanka and I took bits from both and put them together to make 2000 words.'  But the sites said everything so much better than I can... DOWNLOAD whirr Buzz	That's not going to show your learning – even if you might have learned something by finding the sites and deciding what to choose. Plus, if you don't use quotes to show you did not write these words, and you do not say where each idea the reader meets comes from, then that's plagiarism.
'I have written this essay about sustainable tourism in Sri Lanka. I read about sustainable tourism and how it works elsewhere. Then I found out about tourism in Sri Lanka and thought about how they might use some of the approaches worked out in …'	That shows you understand something. You have drawn together information from several sources, understood principles of sustainable tourism, thought about what might and might not work in Sri Lanka, and explained your reasons …

Made by me!

University tutors:

DO NOT expect undergraduates' work to be 'original': meaning something new not known before, adding to the knowledge in the subject.

That is for researchers! ✗

DO expect your work to be unique in the following sense: 'I made this. I read the information and research in books and articles, picked out bits that are useful to me, and used them in my argument or explanation – in my own way, in my own words.' ✓

Good writing is like good cooking. Plagiarism is like microwaving frozen pies.

Good writing	Good cooking
You go to the library or to electronic databases and indices.	You go to the market.
You find lots of sources listed.	You find lots of vegetable stalls.
You choose the best ones, good sources on your topic.	You choose the best stalls and pick the vegetables you want: *Not these, I'll take those.*

Good writing	Good cooking
You write down your ideas and add the ideas from sources. You edit and change and shape the writing.	You chop the ingredients, mix them up, and drop them into the dish at the right time.

The result? Your own work. It's original – not 'brand new' original but 'made by you'.

10 Why show your sources?

The best reasons for showing sources have nothing to do with protecting yourself from accusations of plagiarism. If you are the author, then give yourself credit for the work you have done.

Using sources shows …

1 Evidence

Where you are not a recognised expert, you need others' research and ideas to support your own. It's not just *you* making a claim or stating a fact or suggesting a reason for something – others have researched this, and they provide the evidence for what you are saying.

2 Credibility

The reader can have confidence in your writing because of the type of source you are using. The reader will know that some sources are vetted and tested: for example peer-reviewed journals, books from well-known publishers, tested experimental results, or respected authorities. Other sources of evidence are considered to be weak because there was no quality assurance process before they were published – many websites,

Wikipedia, and popular media. 'Weak' does not mean it isn't true. It means we cannot be confident that it is. Who knows who wrote it? Who checked it?

3 Traceability

If you say where something comes from, readers can check for themselves. Did you get the quote right? Is it true that the experiment had the result you claim? Readers may choose not to check but by providing the option, you show honest and transparent use. It relaxes the reader.

4 Authority

Your references show whether you have been able to find the right sort of sources for this piece of work. Are they evidence-based? Up to date? Well selected from the dozens of similar sources?

5 Reliability

If you show you can use the conventions of quoting, referencing and commenting on others' work in ways that are transparent and careful, the reader gains confidence in your writing overall, seeing it as likely to be an accurate reflection of the sources you have used.

6 Reach and scope

Your sources can make the point that you have been reading widely, looking beyond the predictable textbooks, lecture notes and newspaper stories to see what ideas and evidence are out there and to select the best for this piece of writing.

7 Politeness

Giving credit to others shows you are mindful of their work. It shows you are a respectful member (albeit a junior one) of the subject 'community'. Extend the courtesy to fellow students and acknowledge (see p. 29) their ideas when you draw on them in your own work.

11 Getting help with your work

It has to be 'my own work'. Does that mean no one can help?

Absolutely not! You do not need to do everything yourself. You can and should ask others for help and advice when you need it. But what kind of help?

Here's a simple test about asking for advice: are you asking for advice or help so *you* can do the work? Or do it better? If the answer is 'yes' then that's fine.

Or is the 'help' really about getting someone else to do the work *for* you? This is not OK.

DO ask tutors or university study advisers for advice.

Don't hesitate! Just ask – it's what they are there for.

Getting advice early on is always a good idea – it kick-starts you to understand what the essay or assignment is asking you to do, and planning your work.

What other sorts of help can you use?

1 Help with research

YES

▸ when someone shows you how to locate sources or use databases

▸ if using others' research to trigger your own: for example, tracking down the references from another source.

NO

▸ if it means someone else doing the searching and choosing for you.

2 Help with making notes: 'I used Nick's notes to write my essay'

YES

▸ if you credit Nick for any interpretations he makes of the original (but watch out! Are Nick's notes any good to you? Is he reliable?).

NO

▸ if you use the notes as if you did the original research. This is creating a false impression in your reader that you did the work.

3 Talking to others about your work

YES Definitely!

▶ Discussion is a great way to shape your own ideas. If you are *not* talking to people about your subject, you are really missing out!

And especially YES

▶ when it sends you back to do more thinking and research
▶ or, together, you all create a new, shared idea, approach or project.

NO

▶ if you just swallow other people's ideas and copy them as if they were yours ('without attribution').

[Note: it's polite to name fellow students if they were crucial to your understanding – but do use an informal style such as, 'According to xxx'. A full citation would be weird.]

4 Help with writing up: 'I did the data collection and analysis but she wrote it up for me'

YES

▶ if someone does a bit to show you how to do this sort of writing
▶ if you make it clear to the reader which bits were written by you and which were not.

NO

▶ if you hand over the work of writing to someone else – then it's their work, not yours.

5   Help with proofreading/checking/editing

YES

- if the tutor says you can – do ask!
- if you choose someone who will only correct 'lower-order language issues' – the sorts of things a grammar checker would highlight
- if you are not being graded on accuracy of language
- if you can show the tutor what changes have been made (by handing in 'before' and 'after' drafts, for example).

NO

- if being able to write accurate prose or correct grammar is part of the 'work' being judged
- if your proofreader changes things which mean the marker cannot tell what is your work and what is the proofreader's (by rewriting or making big changes to the structure, for example).

12 What counts as plagiarism?

Below are two quizzes about plagiarism in practice. Have a go!

Quiz 1 is about how students tackle the research for their assignments – what is and isn't acceptable about their approaches.

Quiz 1: Academic integrity at work?

	Question: Does this show 'academic integrity'? (p. 52)	**Answer** Yes/No
1	You have to write a research paper. You read an article which cites other articles that you do not actually read. The author of the article you do read has summarised them. You list both the article you have read and the ones you haven't in your reference list.	
2	You go to an art gallery and make sketches of six pictures, then take elements from each one as inspiration for your own picture. Then you hand in your own.	

Question: Does this show 'academic integrity'? (p. 52)		Answer Yes/No
3	You download 1500 words off the web, make some changes to the examples the web text uses to make the download more relevant to the assignment topic, then hand it in. Luckily, the website has a bibliography too, so you also include this.	
4	You ask someone to proofread and correct your essay before you hand it in.	
5	You write in your own words about a complicated idea you found in a book. You put the full reference for the book in the reference list. There is no indication in your text that this idea comes from the source you list.	
6	The assignment asks for information you can find in a textbook. You copy out the answer, put " … " around the copied text and add the author's name and page after the quote marks.	

Now check your answers with ours shown upside down on the next page.

Answers to Quiz 1: Does this show 'academic integrity'?

1	NO. This breaks the trust that underpins academic work. You haven't clapped eyes on many of the articles you list in your references, and don't really know what they say apart from the summaries of the other author. This is 'fabrication'.
2	YES. This is absolutely fine – it is what all students should be doing in their sketchbooks.
3	NO. Classic plagiarism. Think of all the work that went into the research you are claiming as your own!
4	Tricky. To what extent is it still 'your own work'? If the checker went beyond the kind of tidy-up that computer spell- and grammar-checkers do, it could be plagiarism.
5	NO. You need to show where exactly you drew on someone else's work, and just including the source in the reference list does not do this.
6	YES. But this looks like unconfident writing, and if you do too much of this without commenting on what is important/special/noteworthy about the quote, your own 'voice' won't come through. Make sure you include the full reference in the reference list.

Quiz 2: Which side of the line?

Quiz 2 is about good practice when you describe research in your work. Read the following extract and assess how it is used.

> … We conducted a research project involving 3,300 consumers in 41 countries and found that most people choose one global brand over another because of differences in the brands' global qualities. We recommend companies think about the issue in cultural terms … Popular culture is created and preserved mainly by different forms of communication: newspaper and magazine articles, television and radio broadcasts, Internet content, books, films, music, art, and, of course, advertising and marketing communications. For decades, communication circulated mostly within the borders of countries, helping to build strong national cultures. Toward the end of the twentieth century, much of popular culture became global. As nations integrated into the world economy, cross-border tourism and labor mobility rose; TV channels, movies, and music became universally available to consumers; and, more recently, Internet growth has exploded. Those factors force people to see themselves in relation to other cultures as well as their own. For instance, consumers everywhere have to make sense of the world vis-à-vis Hollywood and Bollywood films, CNN and al-Jazeera news reports, hip-hop and Sufi music.
>
> The rise in global culture doesn't mean that consumers share the same tastes or values. Rather, people in different nations, often with conflicting viewpoints, participate in a shared conversation …

Holt D, Quelch J and Taylor E (2004). How Global Brands Compete. *Harvard Business Review*. Sept. 82(9) p68–75.

Four student writers used the text above in an essay on branding. Decide for each whether the use is the right side or the wrong side of the line between good academic writing and leaning too heavily on someone else's work.

1	No matter where people live, they look at the same media and music such as Hollywood and Bollywood films, CNN and al-Jazeera news reports, satellite TV and hip-hop. The rise of a global culture doesn't mean that consumers share the same tastes or values but one of the key influences in their shopping is the global brand.
2	Holt et al (2004) conducted a survey involving 41 countries to find out how people chose particular products. They make the point that before the end of the Twentieth Century, communication circulated mostly within the borders of countries, helping to build strong national cultures. Now, much of popular culture is global because of cross-border tourism, labor mobility and shared media.
3	Companies in the 21st Century need to be aware of the importance of global brands because shoppers all over the world make decisions based on how they feel about particular brands. National consumer cultures do vary but they are also increasingly similar because '… people in different nations, often with conflicting viewpoints, participate in a shared conversation, drawing upon shared symbols' (Holt et al 2004).
4	If companies that operate around the world want to understand how their customers make decisions, they must think about their brand as global and think of their customers as responding to a host of similar messages and communications from the media, although consumers probably interpret the meanings in different countries in different ways (Holt et al 2004).

This is what we thought about these extracts. How do our views compare with yours?

1	This is too close to the original. In a snippet like this, the copying is probably not noticeable but it may be a dangerous habit and, used widely in an assignment, will definitely cause trouble.
2	This writer uses the article to start creating his/her own message and cites it well, then falls back on too much copying. Did you notice how the cut-and-paste strategy left in an American spelling ('labor')? The reader will definitely notice and will start to wonder whose work this is.
3	Nice. It might be better to comment on why the Holt et al quote is used. Is it particularly vivid? There is no page number since it comes from a web version. You could track down the page number in the printed version but, really, your time is better spent doing more writing and thinking. This is fine.
4	Summary rather than paraphrase – a good idea. Also, the ideas are close to 'common knowledge', but by adding the citation the writer shows that some fairly authoritative people think so, too.

You know when work you hand in is your own because you
▸ know where the ideas came from
▸ know where the words came from

and show your reader with your in-text referencing links (citations) and the full reference details. Plus, you
▸ know that your work is 'made by you'. You are the author.

Your reader can tell if it's your work …

Tutors find it easy to see where students have lifted words from someone else and spliced chunks of text together. These are some of the tell-tale signs:
▸ style changes: the language used by student writers, published writers and random web sources is usually quite different
▸ a mix of referencing systems (some numeric, some author-date, some with no references at all)
▸ oddities in expertise – say, when a complicated problem or very advanced methodology is dropped into a piece of work without explanation.

The electronic text matcher can tell …

Universities increasingly use text-matching software such as Turnitin to identify when students include extracts of other texts. Finding that your text matches something else isn't necessarily a bad thing – when you quote, or use standard introductory phrases, it may well show up as a match, and that's fine. But because these software packages show matches of text, they can also help tutors detect plagiarism.

Some universities and courses allow students to check their work using Turnitin, or use it as part of the process of submitting work electronically. If you get the chance to do this, think of it as a friendly proofreader inviting you to say, 'Yeah, that's fine' or 'OK, I'll look at that again'. It's a machine, not a fly-trap!

How Turnitin works

- ▶ It turns your text into digital chunks and sees if the chunks match the texts in millions of students' previous work in the Turnitin database.
- ▶ It checks for matches on the web and in a limited range of paper-based sources.
- ▶ It reports the sources and the percentage from each in your text.

Each report needs checking by a tutor to make sense of it. Universities that use Turnitin usually train tutors in how to interpret reports so that they don't automatically assume that any particular percentage of match suggests plagiarism.

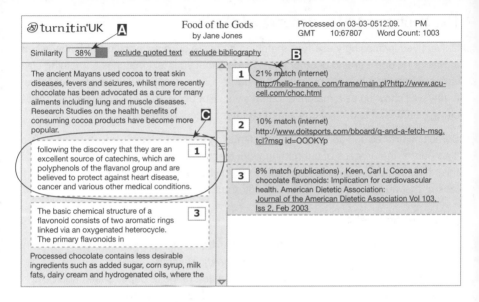

Similarity [38%] excute quoted text excute bibliography [B]

The ancient Mayans used cocoa to treat skin diseases, fevers and seizures, whilst more recently chocolate has been advocated as a cure for many ailments including lung and muscle diseases. Research Studies on the health benefits of consuming cocoa products have become more popular. [C]

1 following the discovery that they are an excellent source of catechins, which are polyphenols of the flavanol group and are believed to protect against heart disease, cancer and various other medical conditions.

3 The basic chemical structure of a flavonoid consists of two aromatic rings linked via an oxygenated heterocycle. The primary flavonoids in

Processed chocolate contains less desirable ingredients such as added sugar, corn syrup, milk fats, dairy cream and hydrogenated oils, where the

1 21% match (internet)
http://hello-france. com/frame/main.pl?http://www.acu-cell.com/choc.html

2 10% match (internet)
http://www.doitsports.com/bboard/q-and-a-fetch-msg.tcl?msg id=OOOKYp

3 8% match (publications) , Keen, Carl L Cocoa and chocolate flavonoids: Implication for cardiovascular health. American Dietetic Association: Journal of the American Dietetic Association Vol 103, Iss 2, Feb 2003

A – *This gives the overall percentage of the text that matches the databases.*

B – *This says how much of the student's text came from this site.*

C – *This shows the match in the student's text so the teacher can see how it is being used.*

The remedy: become a writer

A writer's work is transparent: it shows the writing process.

A student writer relies on others' credibility and authority: referencing shows this has happened.

A good student writer uses the writing process to make sense of all the work that went into that assignment or piece of coursework. This shows you understand what you are writing about.

Good student writing shows the student's learning. You write what you know and know what you are writing about.

It works best if you don't just try and follow the rules but if you understand and believe in the ideas that lie behind the rules. Good student writers never need to worry about plagiarism.

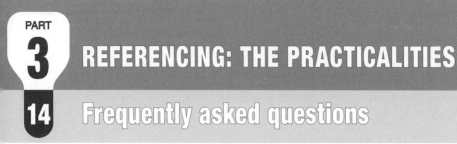

14 Frequently asked questions

References or bibliography? What's the difference?

The **reference list** is a list of all the sources you have referred to in your writing. This is what most tutors require.

A **bibliography** is a list of everything you have read on a subject, including background reading, whether you refer to it or not. You may occasionally be asked for a bibliography – for example when your tutor wants to see where you have got to in your research for a dissertation proposal.

If you are asked for a bibliography for a finished piece of work, divide it into two sections:

1 *References* – for sources you cite in your text
2 *Other sources consulted* – for materials you have read but chose not to use.

Tutors sometimes use the term 'Bibliography' to mean 'Reading list' or 'Suggested reading'.

Should I use reference management software?

It's up to you. University libraries will have some available free to students (like Endnote); others are free to any user (like CiteULike). Give it a try – many students find it invaluable. Others prefer to copy and paste references (try to avoid retyping URLs), or use cards.

For an overview of the various types of software available see Wikipedia: http://en.wikipedia.org/wiki/Comparison_of_reference_management_software

How do I reference a source I found in a book/article but I haven't actually read it myself?

The answer is simple. You don't list something in your references if you haven't actually read it. You list the text where *you* found it in your references list, and show this in your text.

Primary sources are written by the person or organisation who carried out the work themselves, at first hand: data collection, case study, theory, analysis.

Secondary sources are written by someone who has read the primary source and described it in some way. A book or article that refers to or summarises other studies is a 'secondary source'.

See, for example, the following:

In your work you write:	In your references you list:
Herzberg's two-factor theory of motivation at work (Herzberg, Mauser and Synderman 1959 cited in Mullins 1998 p98) clearly shows …	Mullins L (1998). *Managing people in the hospitality industry.* 3rd edition. Harlow: Longman.

It is good practice to use primary sources wherever you can, and be careful about relying too heavily on secondary sources. A textbook or article that summarises a lot of work in the field is a good place to start for an overview. However, if you don't go and find the actual texts, your understanding of the study, data or whatever is limited to the short summary you find in the textbook. You then have to paraphrase someone else's summary (see p. 36).

However, when the original is hard to find (eg, it is old, or has restricted circulation) and you want to use it because it is special in some way (perhaps the author made a real contribution to the field), do so as above.

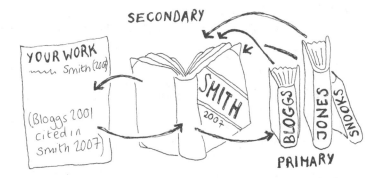

REFERENCING AND UNDERSTANDING PLAGIARISM

When do I put in page numbers?

The test is simple: if what you are referring to came from a particular page, then give the page number. It makes it easier for the reader to pinpoint, and shows how organised you are as a researcher.

▶ Any quote will come from a particular page, so give the page number(s) (see p. 31–2).
▶ If the point you are explaining (summarising or paraphrasing) comes from a particular page, then give the page number(s) (see p. 35).

If you are referring to a general idea, or summarising a whole section or chunk, then don't give the page.

Why do authors put in a string of references?

You are most likely to see this at the beginning of an article, in the introduction. The authors may want to refer briefly to well-established research findings, and then to move on swiftly to the issues that concern them.

Example:

> ... Very few men in Botswana enrolled in home economics programmes in schools and colleges (Smith 2000; Lawson 1998; Fisseha et al 1997).

Or they may want to give an overview of research on different aspects of the topic before they move on to their focus:

> Dispersal is widely recognised to be a key process in ecology, evolution and conservation biology (Clobert et al 2001, Bullock et al 2002). Numerous empirical studies have focussed on ... (Stenseth and Lidicker 1992, Bowne 2004, Martin et al 2004) ... or on distances covered (Wilson 2003, Colbert and Lack 2005) ...

This section gives examples of references from the most frequently used sources: journal articles, books and internet sources.

How to reference a journal article

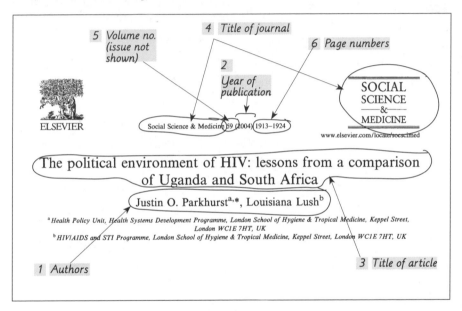

5 Volume no. (issue not shown)

4 Title of journal

6 Page numbers

2 Year of publication

Social Science & Medicine 59 (2004) 1913–1924

ELSEVIER

SOCIAL SCIENCE & MEDICINE

www.elsevier.com/locate/socscimed

The political environment of HIV: lessons from a comparison of Uganda and South Africa

Justin O. Parkhurst[a],*, Louisiana Lush[b]

[a] Health Policy Unit, Health Systems Development Programme, London School of Hygiene & Tropical Medicine, Keppel Street, London WC1E 7HT, UK
[b] HIV/AIDS and STI Programme, London School of Hygiene & Tropical Medicine, Keppel Street, London WC1E 7HT, UK

1 Authors

3 Title of article

The six points of a journal reference	The reference for this article
1 The **author**(s) in the order they are given in the article. Family name (surname) first, followed by their initial(s).	Parkhurst JO and Lush L (2004). The political environment of HIV: lessons from a comparison of Uganda and South Africa. *Social Science and Medicine*. 59(9) p1913–24.
2 The **year** the article was published (in brackets).	If found online add:
3 The **full title** of the article.	Available at: http://www.sciencedirect. com [Accessed 22 July 2008]
4 The title of the **journal** in *italics*.	
5 The **volume** and **issue** (where given).	
6 The **pages** of the article.	

Journal article references

Do you include the URL? It depends how you found the article. If you found it on the shelf in hard copy, then don't include the URL. If you found it via an online database, then include it. The second example below was on the shelf, and the others found via an online database. Add URLs and the date accessed.

In your work	In your references
One author	
Dovlo (2007) describes the impact of …	Dovlo D (2007). Migration of nurses from sub-Saharan Africa: a review of issues and challenges. *Health Services Research.* 42 p1373–88. Available at http://ejournals.ebsco.com [Accessed 27 July 2008]
Two authors	
Uganda was not notably advanced beyond its neighbours (Parkhurst and Lush 2004).	Parkhurst JO and Lush L (2004). The political environment of HIV: lessons from a comparison of Uganda and South Africa. *Social Science and Medicine.* 59(9) p1913–24.
Three or more authors	
… there has been a 12% reduction in available nurses due to migration (Ross et al 2005).	Ross SJ, Polsky D and Sochalski J (2005). Nursing shortages and international nurse migration. *International Nursing Review.* 52(4) p253–62. Available at http://ejournals.ebsco.com [Accessed 18 July 2008]

Online journals

The articles above exist in hard copy and they can also be found online. Online journals only exist online, so the reference needs to take the reader to the exact page.

In your work	In your references
When tutors proactively contact students to offer advice about resits, they are more likely to pass (Catley and Williams 2007).	Catley P and Williams K (2007). Back from the brink: a lifeline for resit students? *Brookes eJournal of Learning and Teaching.* 1(4) Available at http://bejlt.brookes.ac.uk/vol1/volume1issue4/practice/catley_williams.pdf [Accessed 22 July 2008]

The same author has several publications in the same year

When you want to refer to several articles or documents by the same author all published in the same year, you need to be able to show your reader which is which. This most often happens with:

- a weekly journal when a journalist writes regularly on the same or similar topics;
- a government or official body that issues statements, guidelines, reports or policies on a regular basis, such as the Department of Health (DoH) or Environment Agency.

In your work	In your references
You show which is which by adding a letter to the year of your in-text reference: The Gwesty'r Llew Cochin hotel halved their water use by … (Environment Agency 2007b)	Environment Agency (2007a) … (+ full details) Environment Agency (2007b) *Water resources.* Available at http://www.environment-agency.gov.uk/subjects/waterres [Accessed 13 July 2008] Environment Agency (2007c) … (+ full details)

Page for your notes and references

Practise writing references for journal articles, books and internet sources:

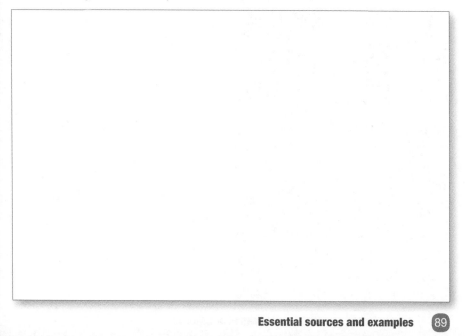

How to reference a book

Books can be written by individuals. Organisations can also be the author.

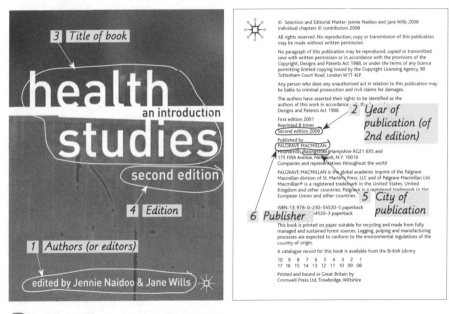

3 *Title of book*

© Selection and Editorial Matter: Jennie Naidoo and Jane Wills 2008
Individual chapters © contributors 2008

All rights reserved. No reproduction, copy or transmission of this publication may be made without written permission.

No paragraph of this publication may be reproduced, copied or transmitted save with written permission or in accordance with the provisions of the Copyright, Designs and Patents Act 1988, or under the terms of any licence permitting limited copying issued by the Copyright Licensing Agency, 90 Tottenham Court Road, London W1T 4LP.

Any person who does any unauthorised act in relation to this publication may be liable to criminal prosecution and civil claims for damages.

The authors have asserted their rights to be identified as the authors of this work in accordance with the Copyright, Designs and Patents Act 1988.

First edition 2001
Reprinted 8 times
Second edition 2008

2 *Year of publication (of 2nd edition)*

Published by
PALGRAVE MACMILLAN
Houndmills, Basingstoke, Hampshire RG21 6XS and
175 Fifth Avenue, New York, N.Y. 10010
Companies and representatives throughout the world

PALGRAVE MACMILLAN is the global academic imprint of the Palgrave Macmillan division of St. Martin's Press, LLC and of Palgrave Macmillan Ltd. Macmillan® is a registered trademark in the United States, United Kingdom and other countries. Palgrave is a registered trademark in the European Union and other countries.

ISBN-13: 978-0-230-54520-5 paperback
ISBN-10: 0-230-54520-3 paperback

5 *City of publication*

6 *Publisher*

This book is printed on paper suitable for recycling and made from fully managed and sustained forest sources. Logging, pulping and manufacturing processes are expected to conform to the environmental regulations of the country of origin.

A catalogue record for this book is available from the British Library

10 9 8 7 6 5 4 3 2 1
17 16 15 14 13 12 11 10 09 08

Printed and bound in Great Britain by
Cromwell Press Ltd, Trowbridge, Wiltshire

health
an introduction
studies

second edition

4 *Edition*

1 *Authors (or editors)*

edited by Jennie Naidoo & Jane Wills

The six points of a book reference	The reference for this book
1 The **name**(s) of the **author**(s) or **editor**(s) in the order they are given on the title page: family name (surname) first, followed by their initials.	Naidoo J and Wills J (eds) (2008). *Health studies: an introduction* (2nd edition). Basingstoke: Palgrave Macmillan.
2 The **year** the book was published. If more than one edition of the book has been published, give the date of the edition you are using.	
3 The **title** of the book in *italics*.	
4 The **edition** of the book in brackets (if shown).	
5 The **city**/town in which the book was published, followed by a colon.	
6 The name of the **publisher**.	

Book references

In your work	In your references
One author	
The definition of terrorism has developed to include ... (Hoffman 2006).	Hoffman B (2006). *Inside terrorism.* New York: Columbia University Press.
Two authors	
According to Baker and Hart (2008), the four factors that contribute most to ...	Baker M and Hart S (eds) (2008). *The marketing book.* Oxford: Butterworth-Heinemann.
Three or more authors	
Slow-twitch fibres in muscle perform a different function to fast-twitch fibres (Sadara et al. 2008 p1013).	Sadara D, Heller HC, Orian G, Purves W and Hillis D (eds) (2008). *Life: the science of Biology* (8th edition). Gordonsville: Freeman.

A chapter in an edited book

In your text you refer to the author(s) of the source you are using. Your reader looks for this name in your references, and sees the book it is in.

In your work	In your references
The case study used by Ogden (2008 p179) suggests that beliefs about food and the individual's experience of eating are powerful factors in …	Ogden J (2008). Health Psychology. In Naidoo J and Wills J (eds). *Health Studies: an introduction* (2nd edition). Basingstoke: Palgrave Macmillan. pp147–80.

E-books

Someone has to pay for e-books! If your library subscribes, you can access them for free.

In your work	In your references
The advantages of … are … (Kenworthy 2005).	Kenworthy C (2005). *Digital video production cookbook.* Safari Books Online. Available at http://proquest.safaribooksonline.com [Accessed 18 July 2008].

How to reference an internet source

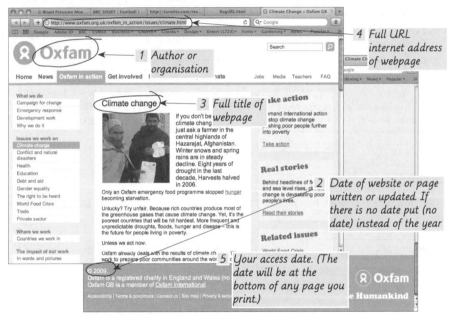

1 Author or organisation

2 Date of website or page written or updated. If there is no date put (no date) instead of the year

3 Full title of webpage

4 Full URL internet address of webpage

5 Your access date. (The date will be at the bottom of any page you print.)

The five points of an internet reference	**The reference for this webpage**
1 The **author**(s) of the website (organisation or person).	*In your work* Cite the webpage in your text as if it was a printed source. Only include the URL in your text if you have no other details:
2 The **year** the website or page was written or updated, if known. (If not known, put 'No date' in brackets).	Oxfam (2008) estimates that 3 billion people in the Middle East and India will suffer from severe water shortages …
3 The **full title** of the webpage or site.	*In your references* Oxfam (2008). Climate change. Available at http://www.oxfam.org.uk/oxfam_in_action/issues/climate.html [Accessed 22 July 2008]
4 The **full internet address** (URL) of the webpage or site.	
5 The **date** on which you accessed the webpage or site.	

You will by now have identified a broad pattern to the information you need to record in a reference for any source you use. You can adapt this to any source you need to reference. Typically it includes:

▶ **Author** (person(s) or organisations)	▶ **Title** of 'host' (eg, book, journal, website, database)
▶ **Year** of publication	
▶ **Title** of item you are reading (eg, book, chapter, article, webpage, website, image, post)	▶ **Helpful details** to locate the text (place of publication, publisher, volume, issue, pages, precise date, format)

And, if it is online, add

▶ The **URL** (internet address/database details)
▶ The **date you accessed** it [Accessed 22 July 2008].

Beyond this, look for models that are as close as possible to what you are looking for. Don't worry about differences in layouts. Present whatever information you can find, in a consistent way. This section includes a few more models you may be able to use and adapt. The point is to be transparent about what your source is, and helpful to your reader if they want to track it. For additional models see your library guides.

Newspapers and magazines

In your work	In your references
Recent research by … suggests that teaching nursery aged children to write simple sentences and read using phonics does not … (Curtis 2008).	Curtis P (2008). Early-years writing lessons 'do no good'. *The Guardian*. July 14 p11. If you find it online via the newspaper's website, add: Available at http://www.guardian.co.uk/education/2008/jul/14//schools.uk [Accessed 24 July 2008]

Brochures and leaflets

In your work	In your references
Recent advice to patients includes revised estimates of units of alcohol in a wineglass (DoH 2008 p9).	Department of Health (2008). *Choices: your health, your choices.* London: The Stationery Office.

Reports and company documentation

In your work	In your references
There has been a marked increase in the numbers of support staff in schools in the last five years (TDA 2007 p5), a trend that …	Training and Development Agency for Schools (2007). *Annual report and accounts 2006–07: developing people, improving young lives.* London: The Stationery Office. If you found it online, add the URL and date you accessed it: http://www.tda.gov.uk/upload/resources/pdf/t/tda_annual_report_2007_web.pdf [Accessed 22 July 2008].

Theses and dissertations

In addition to the standard details, it is helpful to add where the work can be found (eg, a library or collection).

In your work	In your references
The evidence of a link between nutrition and … was explored by Powell (2007) in …	Powell J (2007). Diet and disorder: a review of studies of nutrition and antisocial and criminal behaviour in children and young people. MSc thesis. Oxford Brookes University, Harcourt Hill Library. *Note*: italics are not normally used for the titles of unpublished dissertations and theses.

Course materials

Lecturers prefer you not to reference course materials (eg, lect...
because they want you to use them as a point of departure...
some of their suggestions. But if you do use these as you...
so – it is misleading not to.

In your work	In your referen...
Lecture	
In this case study of Café Direct, I use the principles of … proposed by Grebenik (2008) as a framework for …	Grebenik D (2008). *Ethical business*. ... U61321, Business in context, Week 5. Business School, Southern University.

Audio visual material

TV and radio

In your work	In your references
The poor air quality reported in Beijing (Panorama 2008) is one consequence of …	Panorama (2008). *BBC1*. 14 July.

	In your references
works through ... ...ation. In *Secrets and Lies* ...he ...	*Secrets and lies* (1996). Directed by Mike Leigh [Video]. London: CIBY 2000 in association with Channel 4.

Personal communications

You may need to reference communications you have had with people – for example if you invite comments by email, or carry out a telephone interview as part of a project. You can also include a printed email or letter as an appendix. Don't take this to extremes – if your reader really can't track back to your source, and you don't need to supply evidence of what you did, there's not much point detailing it.

In your work	In your references
FitzGerald (2009) offered some additional insights into ...	FitzGerald J (2009). Conversation [or letter/email/phone conversation] with/to Brenda Laycock, 13 April.

Blogs

Blogs (weblogs) are in effect open conversations online between anyone who cares to join in. They are a useful source of up-to-the min illustration and debate. Postings use aliases, can be removed, amended at any time, so you cannot use them as 'evidence' of anything other than wh are – an online conversation between people you don't know. If you refer to a b include any helpful details. The date you accessed it is essential.

In your work	In your references
In the discussion about the methods by which the British Crime Survey is complied, Gomer (2008) observes …	Gomer (2008). Knife crime: what is the truth? *Guardian newsblog*. Comment No. 1224803. July 17 14:37. Available at http://blogs.guardian.co.uk/news/2008/07/crime_is _down_but_what_about_k.html#comments [Accessed 22 July 2008].

to the most obvious differences in style and usage in the ... ...es. For specialist referencing styles (eg, OSCOLA in Law) ... ...guides.

... ...rticular style will take you to various university library web-

But be prepared for variations. Even within guidance to the same style, individual course/module handbooks, institutions and journals will have their own 'house styles' too. So:

- get the general idea of how to use a style (from this book)
- find out which style you are asked to use
- find a good set of models
- stick to it for consistency
- and don't worry too much about minor variations and total 'correctness'.

Since the Harvard (author-year) system is used throughout this guide, it is not outlined here.

APA

The APA style of the American Psychological Association is used in some publications in psychology, occupational therapy and related disciplines. It is very similar to Harvard, which is also widely used in these subjects.

In your work	In your references
<ul><li>Cite the author(s) surname(s) + year</li><li>No need to repeat the year when you refer to the same author in the same paragraph</li><li>List up to 6 authors in your in-text citation, before putting 'et al' for additional authors.</li></ul>In study of teenage girls, Sallis & Overs (1999) found that … Sallis & Overs also noted … [Note the preference for '&' not 'and'.]	<ul><li>Arrange in alphabetical order by author</li><li>Use a 'hanging indent', i.e. the first line of each reference goes to the margin – the rest is indented</li><li>Present tables without lines between columns and rows.</li></ul>Sallis, K. & Overs L. (1999). *Physical activity and behavioural medicine.* Thousand Oaks, CA: Sage Publications.

MLA

This style is most used in arts and humanities subjects, where detailed discussion of text requires precise and repeated referencing, often to specific quoted phrases. The in-text reference gives the author's name and the page referred to, not the year of publication. This is normally enough to find the full details of the publication in the 'Works cited' at the end.

In your work	In your references or 'Works cited'
▶ Look carefully at the in-text reference: the author's name is given, with the *page number(s)* – not the year of publication.	▶ Use 'Works cited' instead of 'References' for your heading. ▶ List works alphabetically by surname. ▶ Include the first author's first name in full (not just the initial). ▶ The title of the book or journal is underlined, or, increasingly, in italics. ▶ The year of publication is at the end of the reference.
…. Tiller argues that the text 'poses some difficult questions …' (357).	Tiller, Susan. *Mrs Dalloway and London.* London and Los Angeles: University of California Press, 1998.
Claire Levenson (43–44) comments on the 'real world' of wartime Britain in which …	Levenson, Claire. 'Women in the War Years'. <u>Virginia Woolf and the War; Fiction and Reality.</u> Ed. Michael Cramer, 30–45. New York: Methuen, 1999.

Numeric (British Standard)

This style is most commonly used in science, medicine and related subjects. It focuses the reader's attention on the research (which is fully identified in the 'references' section at the end), and is economical with the word count!

In your work	In your references
▶ Use a number in brackets, round (12) or square [12], or in superscript[12] to make the link with the full reference at the end.	▶ References are listed in the order you draw on them in your text, starting from[1] or [1].
▶ The first source you refer to is (1) and so on.	▶ The year goes at the end of the reference before the page number or URL for online sources.
▶ You can use the same number more than once to refer to the same source.	▶ The title of the journal or book is in italics.
▶ You can refer to more than one source if you are using them to support the same point.[22,23]	▶ There is some variation in how many names you list before putting 'et al.'. Six authors is a reasonable cut-off point.

Example:

In your work	In your references
In sub-Saharan Africa, [numbers of] nurses have declined substantially in recent years because of migration. In 2000, roughly 500 nurses left Ghana, double the number of nursing graduates for that same year.[13] The recent upsurge in migration has affected the ability of nurse training programmes to continue because of poor staffing levels.[14] Death caused by infectious and chronic diseases[15] is also a major contributor to nurse attrition in the region. (adapted from Mills et al. 2008)	13 Awases M, Gibary A, Nyoni J and Chatora R. *Migration of health professionals in six countries: a synthesis report.* Brazzaville: World Health Organisation, Regional Office for Africa, 2004. 14 Dovlo D. Migration of nurses from sub-Saharan Africa: a review of issues and challenges. *Health Services Research,* 2007. **42**:1373–88. 15 Tawfik L, and Kinoti S, for USAID. *The impact of HIV/AIDS on health systems and the health workforce in Sub-Saharan Africa.* 2003. Available at http://ftp.info.usaid.gov/our_work/global _health/pop/news/hcdworkforce.doc [Accessed 13 November 2007]

Running notes

This is a distinctive style, used especially in the arts and humanities where interpretation is the substance of the writing. Sources are shown in footnotes on the page (or at the end of the chapter or book as endnotes), along with comments about sources and debates – and it all contributes to the discussion. Sometimes a 'bibliography' is also included at the end, collecting together all the references distributed through the footnotes in the book or article.

This example has been written to show how this referencing style works. It is not a good piece of writing, and has far too many references!

In your work

The popularity of the cinema peaked in the 1940s and 1950s.[1] It remained above 10 million between 1940 and 1955.[2] Precise figures about audiences are hard to come by,[3] but it is clear that the majority of cinema-goers were women.[4] Hollywood carried out research that established that women wanted 'good character development' and 'human interest'.[5] The films produced by Hollywood at this time were 'strongly feminised'[6] and appealed to their largely female audiences for their 'glamour'[7] … Some women watched particular films – such as *Calamity Jane* – countless times …[8]

In your footnotes (or endnotes)	... explained!
1 Pat Fisher, *The Cinema Compendium*, London: British Film Association, 1989, p. 212.	Full details of the source.
2 Ibid., p. 209.	'Ibid.' is short for Latin *ibidem* – 'in the same place'. It refers to the source immediately before (Fisher).
3 For a useful collection of 'facts and figures' of cinema-going Britain, see [source]. The collection of data …	This is a short discussion of the difficulties of finding reliable information – and refers the reader to a book listed in the bibliography at the end of the book.
4 *The Cinema Compendium*, p. 225.	This is a quick referral back to a source already cited in full.
5 Ibid., p. 220.	This refers to *The Cinema Compendium* again. See above for full details.
6 Frank Dubon, *Hollywood Revisited*, London: Studio Panorama, 1994, p. 158.	Another source, full details.
7 Ibid., p. 167.	This refers to the source immediately above – Dubon.
8 These films have provoked considerable debate amongst …	This is the beginning of a lengthy note summarising the discussion amongst commentators.

References

Department of Health (2008). *Healthy weight, healthy lives: a cross government strategy for England.* Available at http://www.dh.gov.uk/en/Publicationsandstatistics/Publications/PublicationsPolicyAndGuidance/DH_082378 [Accessed 27 June 2008]

Eriksen TH (1993). *Ethnicity and Nationalism: Anthropological Perspectives.* London: Pluto Press.

Mills EJ, Schabas WA, Volmink J, Walker R, Ford N, Katabina E, Anema A, Joffres M, Cahn P, Montaner J (2008). Should active recruitment of health workers from sub-Saharan Africa be viewed as a crime? *The Lancet.* 371, Feb. 23, pp685–88.

Neville C (2007). *The complete guide to referencing and avoiding plagiarism.* Maidenhead: Open University Press.

Ofsted (2008). *Schools and sustainability. A climate for change?* Available at http://www.ofsted.gov.uk/assets/Internet_Content/Shared_Content/Files/2008/may/schoolsandsustain.doc [Accessed 27 June 2008]

Orwell G (1946). Politics and the English language. *The collected essays, journalism and letters of George Orwell. Vol. 4: In front of your nose 1945–1950.* Penguin Books: Harmondsworth, pp156–70.

Useful sources

LearnHigher has compiled a list of useful sources of advice and models for referencing in a range of styles:

http://www.learnhigher.ac.uk/learningareas/referencing/resourcepage.htm

Pears R and Shields G (2010). *Cite them right: the essential referencing guide* (8th edition). Basingstoke: Palgrave Macmillan.

This is a great guide to referencing all sorts of sources.

Portsmouth University has an interactive guide to the main referencing styles which provides a tailored model in three clicks:

http://referencing.port.ac.uk/index.html

Most UK universities have webpages with advice on referencing and plagiarism and how to avoid it – check yours. Look at some of the links.

The *Acknowledgement* site in Australia offers a wide range of guidance to teachers and students, including several online quizzes.

http://calt.monash.edu.au/staff-teaching/plagiarism/acknowledgement/about/index.html

Index

Loughborough
COLLEGE

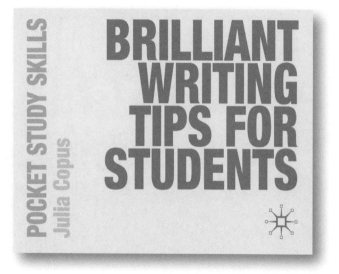

POCKET STUDY SKILLS

Julia Copus

BRILLIANT WRITING TIPS FOR STUDENTS

POCKET STUDY SKILLS

Kate Williams

GETTING CRITICAL

PLANNING YOUR ESSAY

POCKET STUDY SKILLS

Janet Godwin

BLOGS
WIKIS
PODCASTS
& MORE

POCKET STUDY SKILLS

Andy Pulman